the lost words

A Spell Book

Jackie Morris grew up in the Vale of Evesham and studied at Hereford College of Arts and at Bath Academy. She has illustrated for the *New Statesman*, *Independent* and *Guardian*, collaborated with Ted Hughes, and has written and illustrated over forty books, including beloved classics such as *The Snow Leopard*, *The Ice Bear*, *Song of the Golden Hare*, *Tell Me a Dragon*, *East of the Sun*, *West of the Moon* and *The Wild Swans*. Jackie Morris lives in a cottage on the cliffs of Pembrokeshire.

the
lost
words

A Spell Book

ROBERT MACFARLANE

JACKIE MORRIS

HAMISH HAMILTON
an imprint of
PENGUIN BOOKS

ROBERT MACFARLANE

For Lily, Tom, Woffle and other animals.

JACKIE MORRIS

For Ann Humble, who loves the names of things and knows the importance of naming. And for Andreas, who loves goldfinches and Ann.

Once upon a time, words began to vanish from the language of children. They disappeared so quietly that at first almost no one noticed – fading away like water on stone. The words were those that children used to name the natural world around them: acorn, adder, bluebell, bramble, conker – gone! Fern, heather, kingfisher, otter, raven, willow, wren . . . all of them gone! The words were becoming lost: no longer vivid in children's voices, no longer alive in their stories.

You hold in your hands a spellbook for conjuring back these lost words. To read it you will need to seek, find and speak. It deals in things that are missing and things that are hidden, in absences and in appearances. It is told in gold – the gold of the goldfinches that flit through its pages in charms – and it holds not poems but spells of many kinds that might just, by the old, strong magic of being spoken aloud, unfold dreams and songs, and summon lost words back into the mouth and the mind's eye.

acorn

acorn

As flake is to blizzard, as

Curve is to sphere, as knot is to net, as

One is to many, as coin is to money, as
   bird is to flock, as

Rock is to mountain, as drop is to fountain, as
   spring is to river, as glint is to glitter, as

Near is to far, as wind is to weather, as
   feather is to flight, as light is to star, as
   kindness is to good, so acorn is to wood.

adder

adder

A hank of rope in the late hot sun; a curl
  of bark; a six, an eight:
    For adder is as adder basks.

Deep in heather, coiled in gorse, sunk among
  the winter stones:
    For adder is as adder hides.

Darts, diamond slides, sine-wave swerves,
  live-wire curves of force:
    For adder is as adder glides.

Echo of snake, self-escape, a left-behind ghost:
    For adder is as adder sheds.

Rustle of grass, sudden susurrus, what
  the eye misses:
    For adder is as adder hisses.

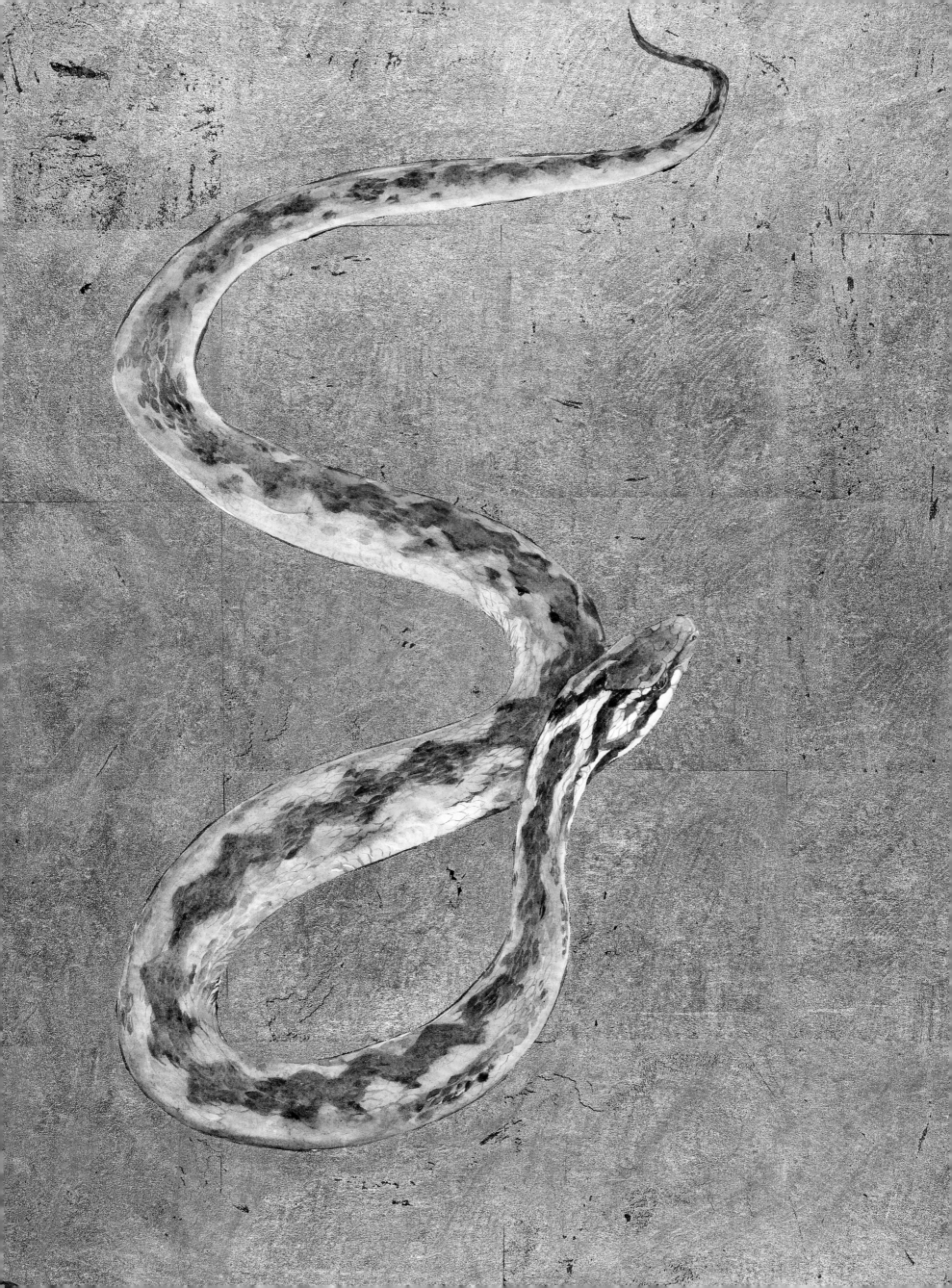

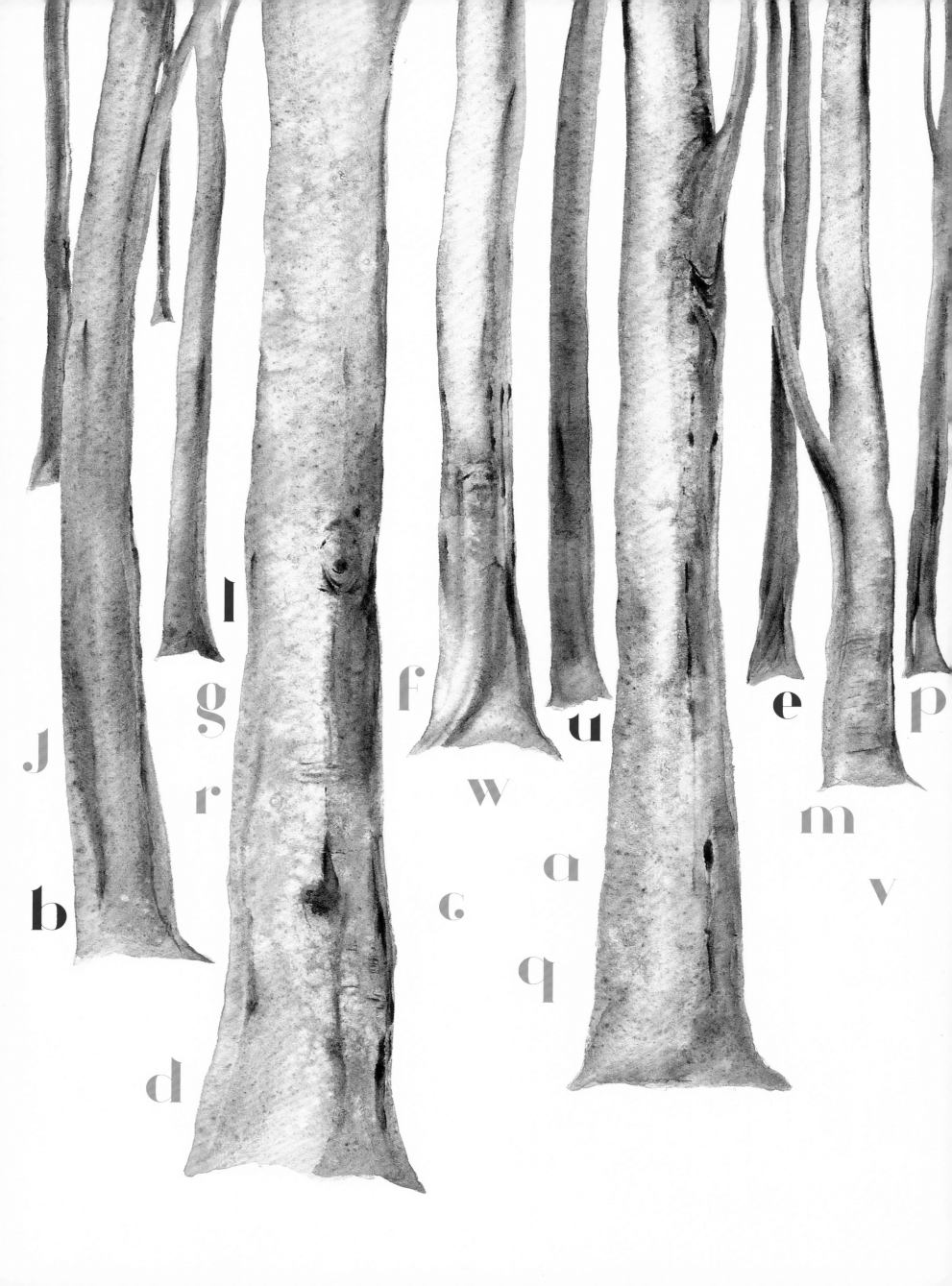

bluebell

---

bluebell

Blue flowers at the blue hour –

Late-day light in a bluebell wood.

Under branch, below leaf,
  billows blue so deep, sea-deep,

Each step is taken in an ocean.

Blue *flows* at the blue hour:
  colour is current, undertow.

Enter the wood with care, my love,

Lest you are pulled down by the hue,

Lost in the depths, drowned in blue.

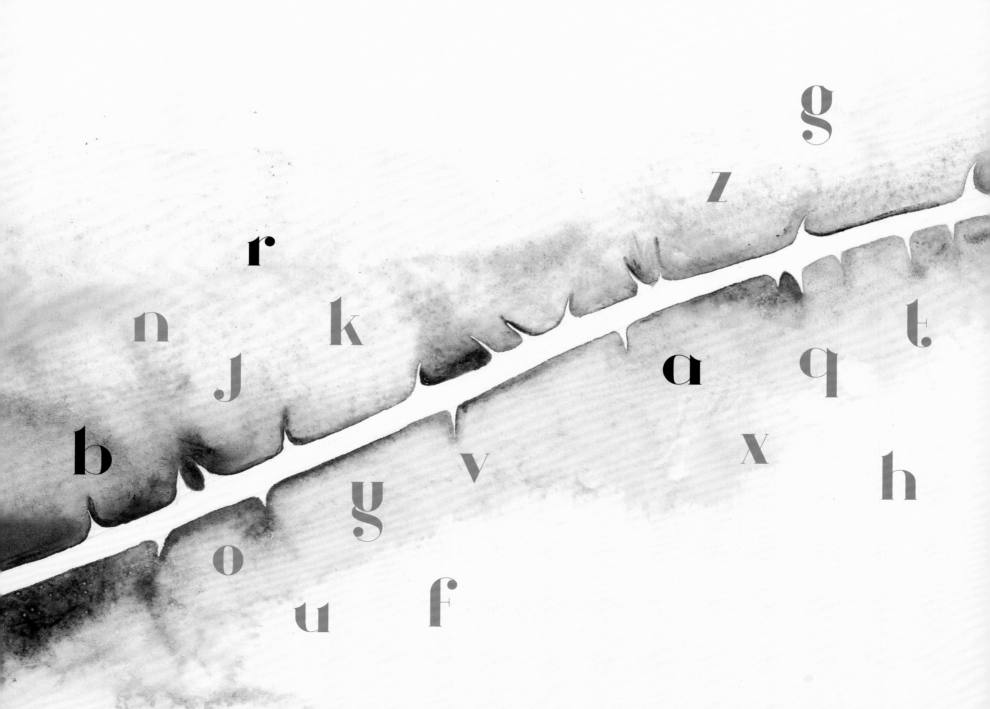

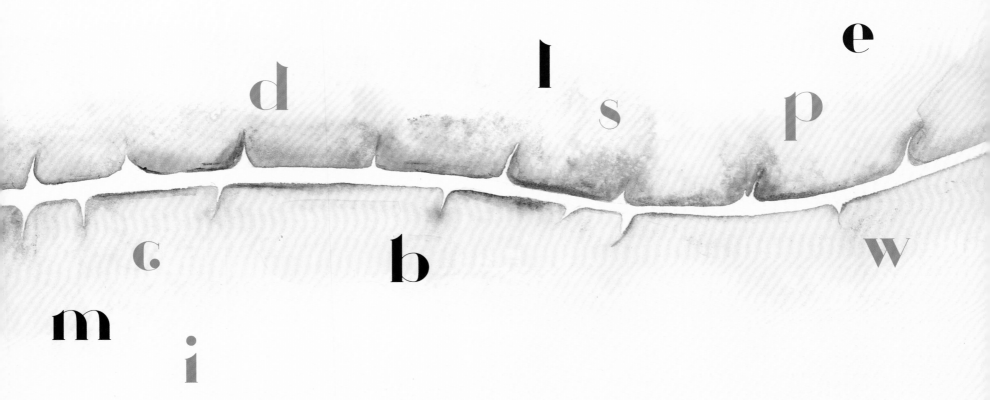

bramble

bramble

B ramble is on the march again,

R olling and arching along the hedges,
    into parks on the city edges.

A ll streets are suddenly thick with briar:
    cars snarled fast, business over.

M oths have come in their millions,
    drawn to the thorns. The air flutters.

B ramble has reached each house now,
    looped it in wire. People lock doors,
    close shutters.

L ittle shoots steal through keyholes,
    to leave – in quiet halls,

E mpty stairwells – bowls of bright
    blackberries where the light falls.

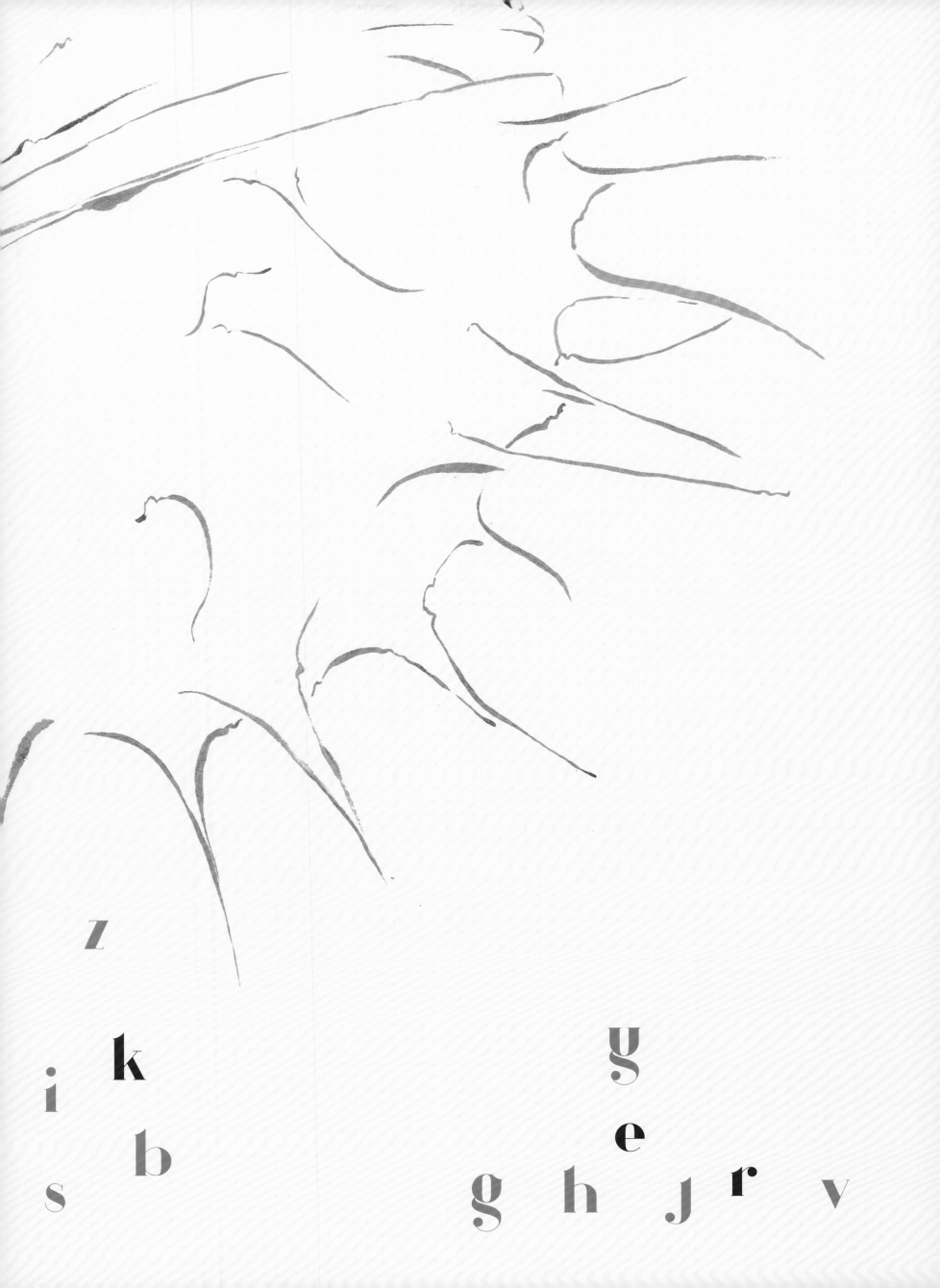

conker

conker

Cabinet-maker, could you craft me a conker?

Oil its wood, burnish its veneer, set it glowing
from within?

Never. Not a chance. No hope at all.

King, then, could you command me a conker?
Compel its green spikes to grow, its white plush
to thicken? *Impossible. Impractical. Inconceivable.*

Engineer, surely you could design me a conker?
Refine its form, mill its curves and edges?
Manufacture me that magic casket?
Unfeasible. Unworkable. Unimaginable.

Realize this (said the Cabinet-maker, the King and
the Engineer together), *conker cannot be made,
however you ask it, whatever word or tool you use,
regardless of decree. Only one thing can conjure
conker – and that thing is tree.*

s

b

d

h

c

m

a

f

p

g   n

w   t

d

j k n u g o v q i r e x l z

dandelion

dandelion

Dazzle me, little sun-of-the-grass!

And spin me, tiny time-machine!
  (*Tick-tock, sun clock, thistle & dock*)

Now no longer known as

Dent-de-Lion, Lion's Tooth or Windblow,
  (*Tick-tock, sun clock, nettle & dock*)

Evening Glow, Milkwitch or Parachute, so

Let new names take and root, thrive and grow,
  (*Tick-tock, sun clock, rattle & dock*)

I would make you some, such as
  Bane of Lawn Perfectionists

Or Fallen Star of the Football Pitch
  or Scatterseed, but

Never would I call you only, merely, simply, 'weed'.
  (*Tick-tock, sun clock, clover & dock*)

b J z e d a f k t h

v q
o n
o r u
p
x
w
g g
i c
m l s

fern

Fern's first form is furled,

Each frond fast as a fiddle-head.

Reach, roll and unfold follows.
  Fern *flares*.

Now fern is fully fanned.

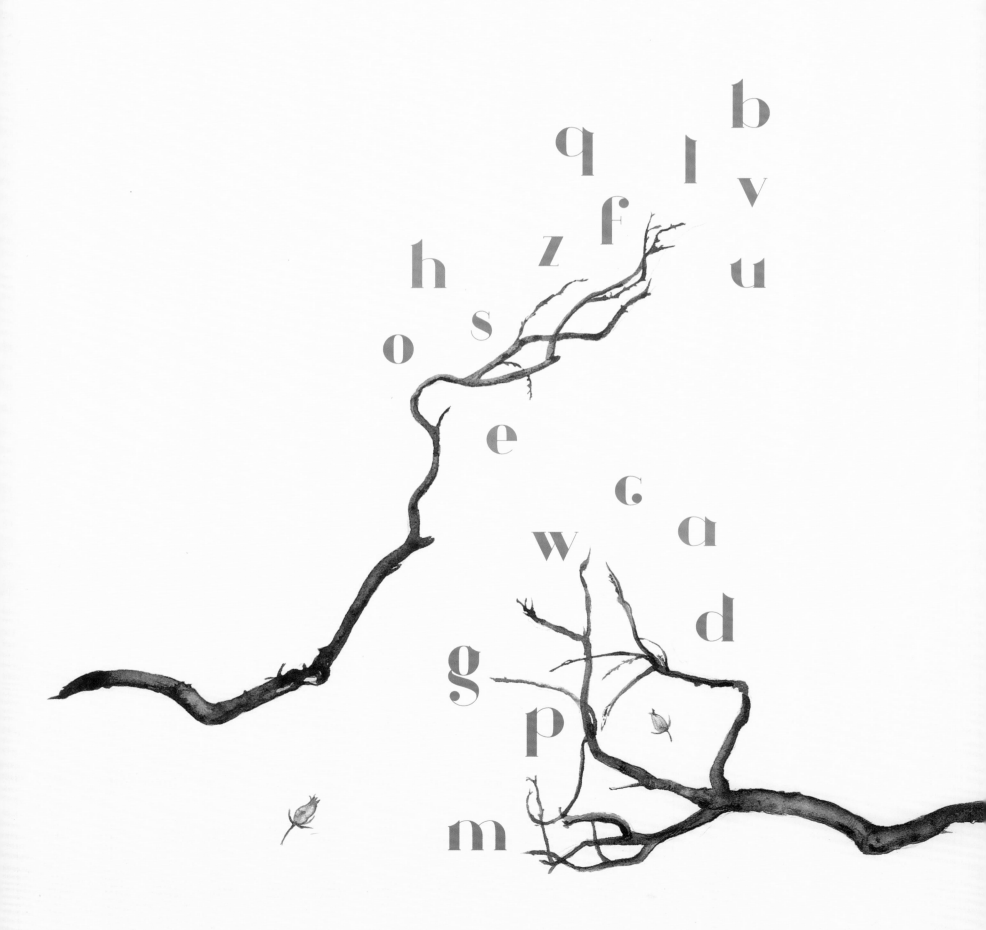

heather

heather

H eather is never only heather,
  as moor is never merely moor.

E ver lain down in heather, got its measure,
  seen how it shares its weather with

A sphodel and bilberry, crowberry and
  cotton-grass, grows together with

T ormentil's flower, moss's cushion,
  lichen's feather?

H old a heartful of heather, never let
  it wither,

E ven as you travel far from crag and river –

R emember heather, the company it keeps,
  its treasure.

a

h

e   f

b

r

o

c

d

q   w

s

p

J   v   n

i

z

g

l

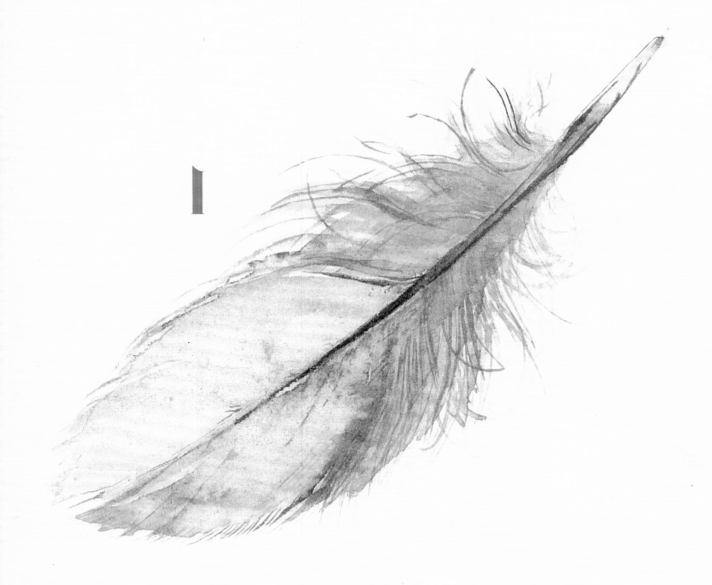

g x m

t

k

u

heron

heron

Here hunts heron. Here haunts heron.
  Huge-hinged heron. Grey-winged weapon.

Eked from iron and wreaked from blue and
  beaked with steel: heron, statue, seeks eel.

Rock still at weir sill. Stone still at weir sill.
  Dead still at weir sill. Still still at weir sill.
  Until, eelless at weir sill, heron magically . . .
  unstatues.

Out of the water creaks long-legs heron,
  old-priest heron, from hereon in all sticks
  and planks and rubber-bands, all clanks and
  clicks and rusty squeaks.

Now heron hauls himself into flight – early
  aviator, heavy freighter – and with steady
  wingbeats boosts his way through evening
  light to roost.

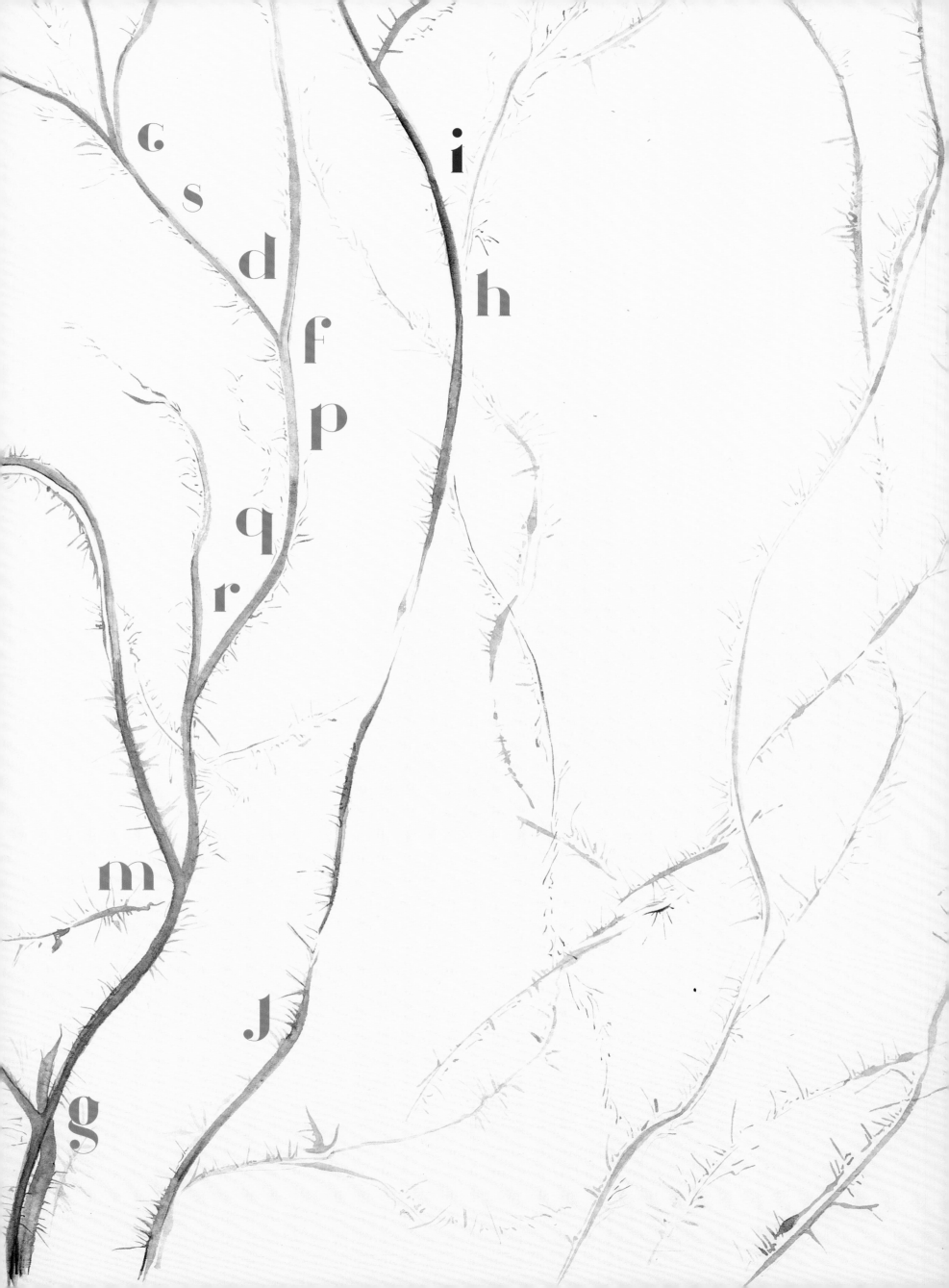

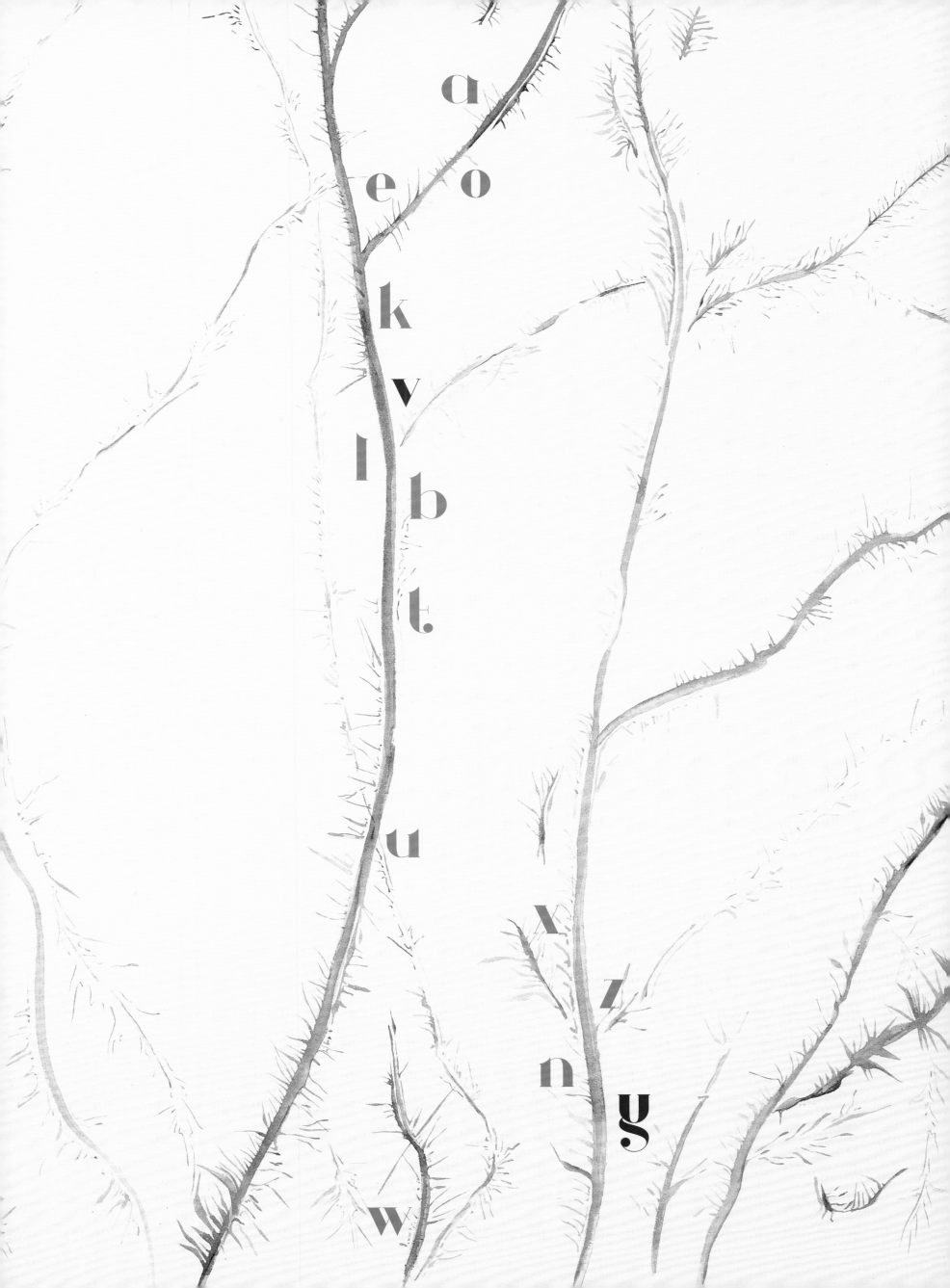

ivy

I am ivy, a real high-flyer.

Via bark and stone I scale tree and spire.

You call me ground-cover; I say sky-wire.

a
l
n
t
b
z
x
v
g
p
d
m
J f
i
s
u
h
c
e r

kingfisher

kingfisher

Kingfisher: the colour-giver, fire-bringer, flame-flicker,
river's quiver.

Ink-black bill, orange throat, and a quick blue
back-gleaming feather-stream.

Neat and still it sits on the snag of a stick, until with . . .

Gold-flare, wing-fan, whipcrack the kingfisher –
zingfisher, singfisher! –

Flashes down too fast to follow, quick and quicker
carves its hollow

In the water, slings its arrow superswift to swallow

Stickleback or shrimp or minnow.

Halcyon is its other name – also ripple-calmer,
water-nester,

Evening angler, weather-teller, rainbringer and

Rainbow bird – that sets the stream alight with burn
and glitter!

d

u

n

h

q

f

z

x   g   t

l   s

m   b

g   a   p   J   w

lark

lark

Little astronaut, where have you gone, and how is your
    song still torrenting on?

Aren't you short of breath as you climb higher, up there
    in the thin air, with your magical song still tumbling on?

Right now I need you, for my sadness has come again
    and my heart grows flatter – so I'm coming to find
    you by following your song,

Keeping on into deep space, past dying stars and
    exploding suns, to where at last, little astronaut,
    you sing your heart out at all dark matter.

magpie

Magpie Manifesto:

Argue Every Toss!

Gossip, Bicker, Yak and Snicker All Day Long!

Pick a Fight in an Empty Room!

Interrupt, Interject, Intercept, Intervene!

Every Magpie for Every Magpie against
  Every Other Walking Flying Swimming
  Creeping Creature on the Earth!

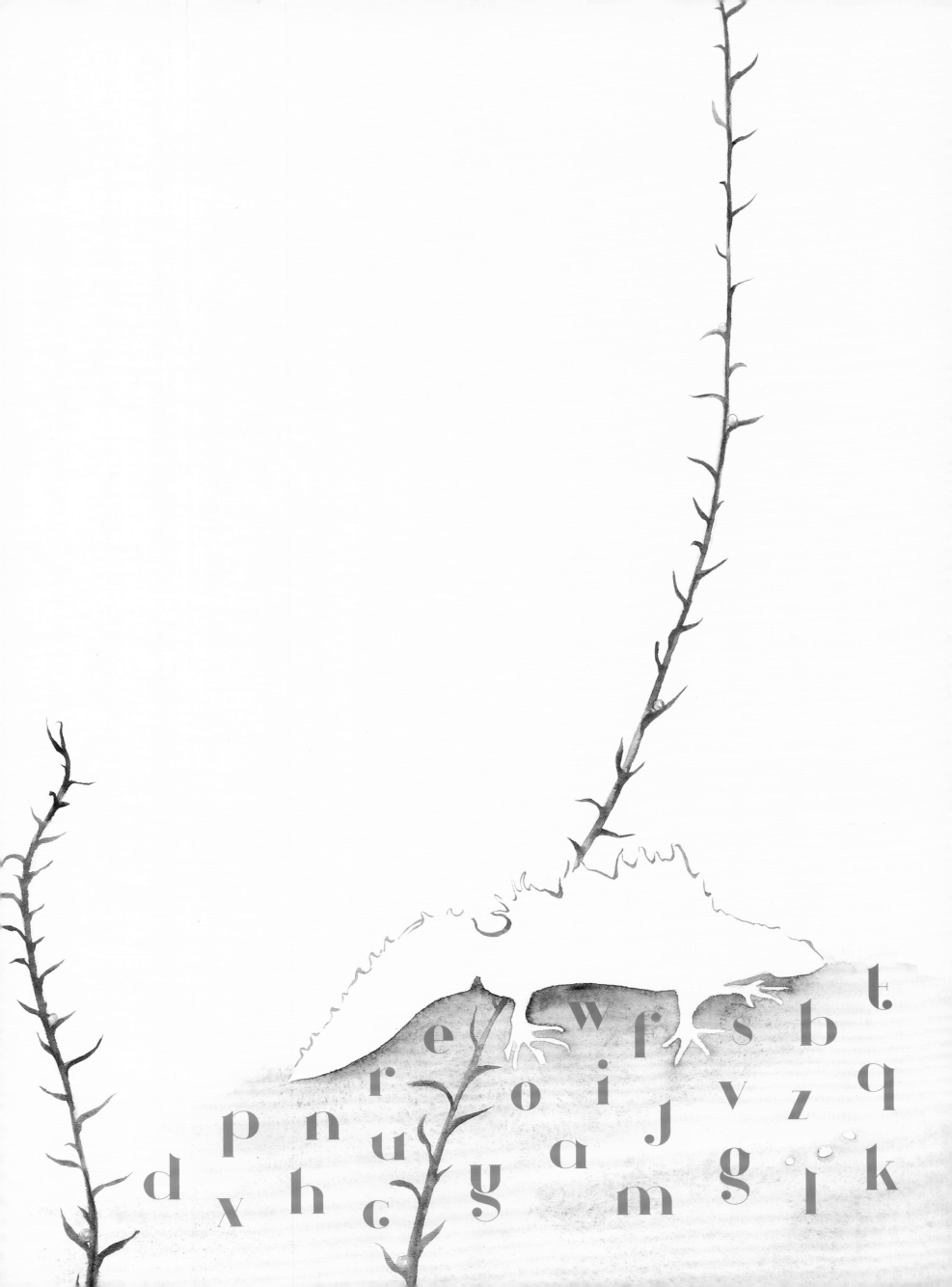

newt

n e w t

'Newt, oh newt, you are too cute!'

Emoted the coot to the too-cute newt,

'With your frilly back and your shiny suit
and your spotted skin so unhirsute!'

'Too cute?!' roared the newt to the
unastute coot. 'With all this careless
talk of cute you bring me into
disrepute, for newts aren't cute:
we're kings of the pond, lions of the
duckweed, dragons of the water;
albeit, it's true,' – he paused – 'minute.'

otter

otter

Otter enters river without falter – what a
supple slider out of holt and into water!

This shape-shifter's a sheer breath-taker, a
sure heart-stopper – but you'll only ever spot
a shadow-flutter, bubble-skein, and never
(almost never) actual otter.

This swift swimmer's a silver-miner – with
trout its ore it bores each black pool deep
and deeper, delves up-current steep and
steeper, turns the water inside-out, then
inside-outer.

Ever dreamed of being otter? That
utter underwater thunderbolter, that
shimmering twister?

Run to the riverbank, otter-dreamer, slip
your skin and change your matter, pour
your outer being into otter – and enter
now as otter without falter into water.

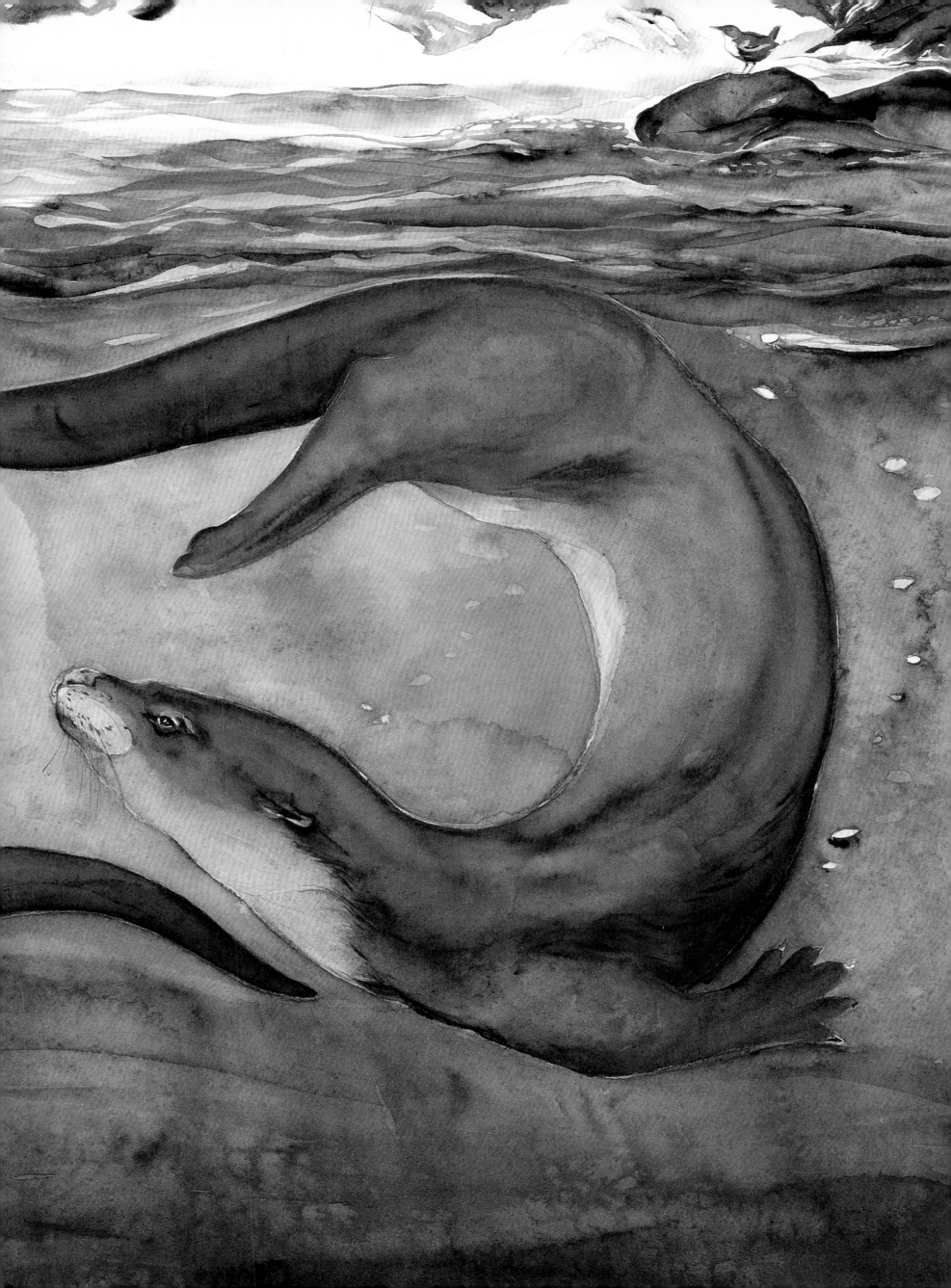

t

r

b

a   x

v

i

s

c

z

g

p f

k

w

q h

g u l m

o n

e J

d

raven

raven

R ock rasps, what are you?

I am Raven! Of the blue-black jacket and the boxer's swagger, stronger and older than peak and than boulder, raps Raven in reply.

A ir asks, what are you?

I am Raven! Prince of Play, King of Guile, grin-on-face base-jumper, twice as agile as the wind, thrice as fast as any gale, rasps Raven in reply.

V ixen ventures, what are you?

I am Raven! Solver of problems, picker of locks, who can often outsmart stoat and *always* out-think fox, scoffs Raven in reply.

E arth enquires, what are you?

I am Raven! I have followed men from forest edge to city scarp: black shadow, dark familiar, hexes Raven in reply.

N othing knows what you are.

Not true! For I am Raven, who nothing cannot know. I steal eggs the better to grow, I eat eyes the better to see, I pluck wings the better to fly, riddles Raven in reply.

c s d   u   a p

q   t o   J   r h l

v   k w   e

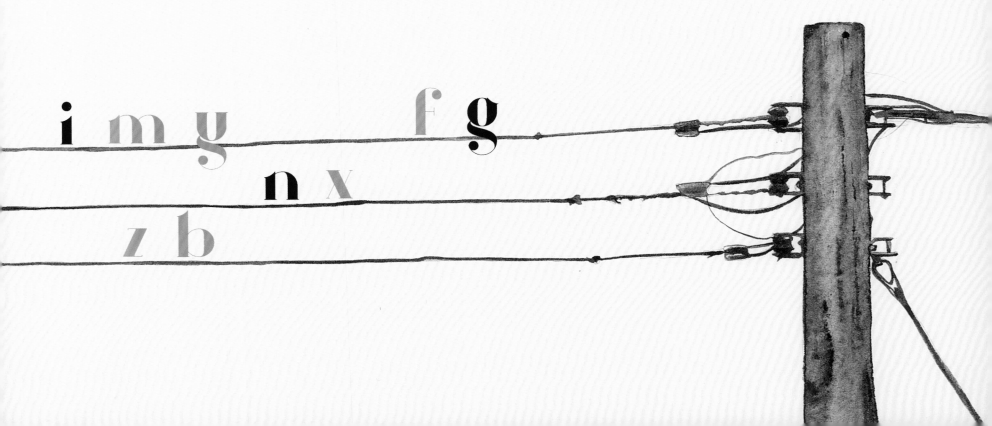

starling

starling

Should green-as-moss be mixed with
  blue-of-steel be mixed with gleam-of-gold
    you'd still fall short by far of the –

Tar-bright oil-slick sheen and
  gloss of starling wing.

And if you sampled sneaker-squeaks
  and car alarms and phone ringtones
    you'd still come nowhere near the –

Rooftop riprap street-smart
  hip-hop of starling song.

Let shade clasp coal clasp pitch
  clasp storm clasp witch,
    they'd still be pale beside the –

In-the-dead-of-night-black, cave-black,
  head-cocked, fight-back gleam of starling eye.

Northern lights teaching shoaling fish teaching
  swarming flies teaching clouding ink
    would never learn the –

Ghostly swirling surging whirling melting
  murmuration of starling flock.

weasel

weasel

Weasel whirls through world like wildfire:

Embers spin, smoke curls, for weasel

Acts on land like spark on tinder –

Scorches grass, turns field to pyre,
  sand to glass, tree to cinder,

Eats air, burns shadow,

Lights the sky, hot-wires the sun with
  its speed, its dance, its gyres.

willow

willow

Willow, when the wind blows so your branches billow,
O will you whisper while we listen so we learn what
words your long leaves loosen?

If you whisper when the wind blows so your branches
billow, willow, we will listen for a day, a week, a year,
till we know what willows say, what willows speak.

*Lean in, listeners, come below our leaves and wait until
the wind blows so our branches billow, listen for a year,
a week, a day, but you will never hear what willows speak,
what willows say.*

*Long you linger, listeners, hard you press your ears against
our bark, but you will never sense our sap, and you will
never speak in leaves, or put down roots into the rot –
for we are willow and you are not.*

O open up your heartwood to us will you, willow, show
your deep within, your rough without, your water-
brushing bough, your shoot, your grain, your knot?

*We will never whisper to you, listeners, nor speak, nor shout,
and even if you learn to utter alder, elder, poplar, aspen,
you will never know a word of willow – for we are willow
and you are not.*

x

v

n

c

e

a

t

wren

wren

When wren whirrs from stone to furze the world around
   her slows, for wren is quick, so quick she blurs the air
   through which she flows, yes –

Rapid wren is needle, rapid wren is pin – and wren's song
   is sharp-song, briar-song, thorn-song, and wren's flight
   is dart-flight, flick-flight, light-flight, yes –

Each wren etches, stitches, switches, *glitches*, yes –

Now you think you see wren, now you know you don't.

HAMISH HAMILTON

UK | USA | Canada | Ireland | Australia
India | New Zealand | South Africa

Hamish Hamilton is part of the Penguin Random House group of companies
whose addresses can be found at global.penguinrandomhouse.com.

First published 2017
001

Printed in China
Colour reproduction by Rhapsody Ltd

A CIP catalogue record for this book is available from the British Library

ISBN: 978-0-241-25358-8

www.greenpenguin.co.uk

A proportion of the royalties from each copy of
The Lost Words will be donated to Action for
Conservation, a charity dedicated to inspiring
young people to take action for the natural world,
and to the next generation of conservationists.
More information on AFC's work with
disadvantaged and socially excluded children can
be found at www.actionforconservation.org.